DRUMMING ARMAGEDDON

Also by George Drew

Toads in a Poisoned Tank

The Horse's Name Was Physics

American Cool

The Hand That Rounded Peter's Dome

The View from Jackass Hill

Down & Dirty

Pastoral Habits: New and Selected Poems

Fancy's Orphan

Chapbooks

So Many Bones (Poems of Russia)

DRUMMING ARMAGEDDON

George Drew

MADVILLE
P U B L I S H I N G

LAKE DALLAS, TEXAS

FIRST EDITION

Requests for permission to reprint or reuse material from this work should be sent to:

Permissions
Madville Publishing
PO Box 358
Lake Dallas, TX 75065

Acknowledgements:

Grateful thanks to the following journals for poems that appeared originally in them:

- *Atticus Review*: "Early Morning at the West Side Y"
- *Chautauqua Literary Journal*: "Easter at the Café Destino" (Part 4 of "Quantum Dickering")
- *Literary Matters (ALSCW)*: "Second Fiddle"
- *The Magnolia Review*: "Don't Blame Me (A Country Tune)"
- *The Schuylkill Valley Journal*: "The Eyes of Frank Orsini," (Part 1 of "Friday Night at Caffe Lena")
- *Stone Canoe*: "Listening to Country on the Tarmac at O'Hare"
- *Vine Leaves Literary Journal*: "Ain't You Lucky?"

And special thanks to Baron Wormser, whose reading of his poem "Jerry Lee Lewis
at Nuremberg" one night in Brattleboro, Vermont inspired the poems in section 2.

For Ken Gaines, Michael Jerling, Rick Kunz, Glenn Raucher, Bob Warren & Claude Wooley, men of
music.

And in memory of Lena Spencer, and in honor of her creation and legacy, Caffe Lena.

Cover Design: Randall Drew
Author Photo: Rick Kunz
ISBN: 978-1-948692-34-2 Paper, 978-1-948692-35-9 ebook
Library of Congress Control Number: 2020936690

I promise to sing while the termite gnaws.

—John Amen

Contents

Drumming Armageddon

1.

THE WORD SWAGGER

Swagger is a nice word most
especially when there is a deficit of swagger.
Swagger is what you crave,
like the full tilt grit of Janis Joplin,
or the guttural smolder of James Brown.
Swagger is a flood of Elvis lookalikes
in Las Vegas—it's that glitzy, that raw.
Swagger is a mouth harp, a fiddle,
it's Ginger Baker in a bluegrass band.
Swagger is getting back your bite
like Jerry Lee after the world
has kicked you in the teeth.
Swagger is a nice word after *good*,
but swagger is even nicer after *bad*.
Swagger is what you have left
when the world has nothing left to give.
Swagger is a bray without a mule.

ON ANOTHER EPIC TRIP AROUND THE SUN

When I turned sixty I was with my kinfolk
in Mississippi, in Grenada, Mississippi to be exact,
boozing it up in a Country Music juke joint.
I was sixty and I was dancing with Jan,
my brother's Queen of the Line Dance wife,
and I was dancing with my once upon a time
Queen of the Jitterbug Aunt Joyce, and more than anyone
I was dancing with my Slow Dance Goddess, Mama.

Now Mama and Aunt Joyce are gone,
my brother's fighting bladder cancer, Jan
nearly died from a bad heart, and she
and my brother don't dance anymore.

And here I am, on the verge of turning three
score and ten in Poestenkill, New York,
and what am I doing?—sitting with my feet up
in front of the tv listening to Emmylou Harris sing
her heart out about Poncho's being laid low.

What's it like? my wiseass friends will ask
tomorrow and for a few tomorrows after that.
Exactly like turning sixty, I'll answer—threats
of absence then, threats of absence ahead.
For now, after Emmylou fades out and credits scroll
down tv screens in Poestenkill, New York,
I'll lift myself from my chair, insert my favorite
Robert Cray cd, and I'll dance. Dance until I drop.

OATMEAL

Outside the New York winter turns the world
white, brownstones burly thugs in the early
morning light, the eight steps leading down
to the Italian bully's slick and treacherous,

and inside up three flights in our apartment
Mama's in the kitchen with the radio set
on Arthur Godfrey playing his stupid ukulele
and like sleet scratching on a window singing,

and Mama warm and doughy as the biscuits
browning in the oven measuring out just
the right amount of sugar, adding in milk,
and stirring oh the little yellow rafts of butter

in the thick and bubbling glop of Quaker's Oats.
Mama in the kitchen getting it right, getting it right.

THE BLUES ARE LIKE A SHOELACE

The blues are like a shoelace,
sometimes double knotted and tight,
sometimes so long and loose
they trip you up, send you sprawling

full out, flat on your shining face.
But that's all right, the blues are about
down not up, about rich and thick,
like Mama's banana cream pudding.

Now I admit, I can't sing the blues,
not a lick, but I love them more
than greens and sweet potatoes, more
than peas bubbling in a big black pot;

I love them more than Daddy's liquor,
and nobody loves his liquor more
than Daddy; hell, I love the blues more
than the Lord on Sunday, more

than women hotter than the Hell
the preacher preaches about,
more even than my old lady; but god
almighty, *please*—don't tell her that.

THE SENSIBLE DADDY BLUES

Son, be like the redtail circling and circling
till it spots its prey, he said, my daddy did,
and then pow! Strike while the striking's hot;

or be like the pilot, he said, my daddy did;
be like the pilot circling the airport far out
from the thunderstorm strafing it with bursts

of lightning and hail until it's safe to land,
and then promptly does, touching down
with everybody on board safe and sound.

He did what he preached, my daddy did,
until at seventy he went under the knife
to have himself repaired, and like a pilot

circling too long and far out from the airport,
he ran out of gas; and even though his
was like the body of a man of forty, down

he came, my sensible daddy did, and now is
nowhere around, not in this, or any other town.

ALBERT AND STEVIE RAY ON PBS

In Session, Dec. 6, 1983

Signifying with his gut-busting grin
and his black face shining with belief,

Albert said Stevie Ray was one picking fool
and that he'd pray, he'd pray for him,

and if he didn't keep on keeping on
he'd whup his Texas backside good,

to which Stevie Ray leaned in and smiled
and let his Fender do his talking for

another seven ripping years, which
after fizzing like a shook-up Coke one

final time and bringing 'em to their feet
with their arms raised, was nothing but

a chunk of wood with metal strings
splattered like Stevie Ray's Texas backside

all over that Wisconsin hill, and Albert,
though he kept his word and prayed, knew

there was no God, there was only the blues,
knew if there was a God, He was the blues,

knew God was the blues, the blues were God,
and God was rocking and God was rolling to

Stevie Ray's last Texas asskicking tune.

SECOND FIDDLE

Mr. Otis has left his home in Georgia,
but why Georgia? And Mr. Brook Benton,
why does he croon about a rainy night
in Georgia? Why has Miz Gladys booked
passage on a midnight train to Georgia?
And then of course there's Georgia Brown.
Why do all these songs cite only Georgia?
Why not Tennessee, or Carolina, or Arkansas?
And why, for god's sake, why not Mississippi?
Why do they all play second fiddle to Georgia?

Must be something about those double g's
snapping fire like Mama's pisselum switch;
must be something about that o and r
lingering like the taste of Granny's buttermilk
on a sizzling Delta day; must be something
about that second syllable dribbling slick
as Aunt Viola's molasses down the chin;
must be something about that trochee
throbbing sweet as one of Georgia's peaches.
Must be something about Georgia. Must be.

LISTENING TO THE BLUES SIX MILES UP

So here you are plugged in and on,
bobbing like a bobber in a fishing hole;
yes, here you are, I say here you are,
grooving to the hot-shit sizzling soul

of Buddy, Robert, Leadbelly, oh,
and Carlos and Mick and Eric, too,
grooving to blues so godalmighty blue
you're turning, I say you're turning blue.

So here you are, I say so here you are
so high you don't know down from up,
your feet, I say your feet, hitting ground
before this badass airplane touches down.

LISTENING TO COUNTRY ON THE TARMAC
AT O'HARE

Uplift—that's what melodic lamentations
in the key of C are meant to provide;
but nothing doing for an hour and a half,
our wings clipped before they even open.

Heartbroken lonesome cowboys soldier on,
their twangs valedictorians of desire,
orators of the down and out lovesick, or
sizzling like Mama's griddle, the one

I'm listening to no different than any other,
just a down-home honky tonk troubadour hunk
making like Merle and Buck and George
here on the rain-riddled tarmac at O'Hare,

most of the songs about Mary or Sue or Molly,
about love lost or love regained or love
never won. Love lost in time and over time,
who sings what beside the point. Like the rider

thrown by a bull, no one remembers him,
only the bull. Uplift—grunts, bucks, snorts.

DON'T BLAME ME (A COUNTRY TUNE)

The devil's getting a bad rap today.
A woman stabs her mother
And it's the devil's doing.
He's inside her, he's taken over.

Honey, next time you give me any lip
I'm gonna sell you down the river.
You deserve it, but even if you didn't
Don't blame me. Blame it on the devil.

The devil's getting a bad rap today.
A mother drowns her children
And it's the devil's doing.
He's inside her, he's taken over.

And if I should ever walk out on you
Without so much as one farewell,
Don't slam the door behind me and curse,
And don't blame me. Blame it on the devil.

The devil's getting a bad rap today.
The children shoot their parents
And it's the devil's doing.
He's inside them, he's taken over.

Oh, and I know what you're thinking:
You'll sue me, take me to the cleaners.
But when I refuse you one red cent
Don't blame me. Blame it on the devil.

The devil's getting a bad rap today.
The parents poison their lovers
And it's the devil's doing.
He's inside them, he's taken over.

And should I ever come begging you
To take me back and you tell me
Not now or ever, and to take a hike,
I won't blame you. I'll blame it on the devil!

The devil's getting a bad rap today.
The lovers burn each other
And it's the devil's doing.
He's inside them, he's taken over.

THE SHERYL CROW I MEAN

And my grandmother, plopped in her recliner
and next to her, her bible; my grandmother,
gentle dumpling of a woman in her eighties
who believed in the Lord, buttermilk biscuits
and crowder peas; my grandmother, velvet Jesus
tacked to the wall and looking down forgivingly
over her shoulder and her head bopping up
and down to Sheryl's certified country licks
and all the while exclaiming *Lord have mercy,*
how that gal can sing; my grandmother, face
puffed into a radiance only the born again
can comprehend and for whom the Sheryl Crow
I mean, the smokin' hot honey dressed in skin
tight black leather pants and matching jacket
and wielding her six-string and harmonica,
meant Mr. Sin and his sidekicks were for
the moment muzzled, her ears closed to them,
pure exultation the coin of her small realm.

MISSING RANDY TRAVIS BY A COUNTRY MILE

It's probably not a good idea to be thinking
about bears when you're lying alone in a cabin
deep in the White Mountains or the Adirondacks,
and definitely not if you're in the Rockies

and the bears are grizzlies, not blacks. *Damn it,*
oh damn it is all you can say, and to escape
turn to the radio and spin the dial to what
you thought was country but turns out not

to be a good idea either, not when you expect
Randy or Dwight and get Ozzie or Michael.
Whatever you do, avoid Black Sabbath,
and for godsakes, don't drift off to "Thriller."

EASTER AT THE CAFÉ DESTINO

For John Dodge

1
Hit them hard, bomb them back
into the Stone Age, nukes on top
of nukes, decimate the commie creeps
once and forever—that was the plan,
that was the mother of all wars,
bouncing the rubble into no-rubble,
radioactive motes of nothing. Dust.

2
From his stool tucked in a corner
of the small café, the guitarist hits
them hard, chord after chord
sharp, blasting the blues away,
collapsing sadness into rubble,
Bach after Bach bouncing the rubble
into radioactive motes of joy.

FRIDAY NIGHT AT CAFFE LENA

1: *The Eyes of Frank Orsini*

If they are pools, I want to dive
in and come up shining
like a big green lily pad on a blue June day.

I've never seen their color:

in the false dawn of the stage
they are sandbagged against a rising river.

I think they're blue.

His bow the smoking cricket's leg
I imagine as he strokes
the high notes of an old time tune,

they open out into an oracle,
each an omen glinting in blue water.

If they are pools, I want to rest
on their edges croaking
in an undreamt key, Joy jumping like a trout.

2: *The Eyes of Mark Patton*

They're the icy blue of choppy water
locked for the winter under ice.
As he powers his guitar strings
you can see the fisherman

red-faced in the wind

propelling himself like a skater out
to the edge of thin ice,

his hands like ivory blossoms
adrift in the brown pool of wood.

Every so often his hands cease
their muscular fluttering

and float like white shadows
toward the glitter of blue holes.

Every so often the red flags trip.

PETER THE MAGIC SEER

Yes! It was him, Peter the six-string seer
Still making magic after all those years.
It was him, Peter Yarrow in the flesh
Arriving on a jet plane. How I gushed.

But on the long drive west to Kerrville
The maestro did nothing but huddle
On his phone with his girlfriend, not
Saying a word to me. And that was that.

Yes! It was him, Peter the six-string seer
Still making magic after all those years,
Not by the sea in the land of Honalee,
But under the tents in Texas Hill Country.

I was dismayed, whatever magic there was
Blown away by his girlfriend and him
And the hot Texas wind, whatever dreams
Remained, mere specks of Texas lint.

Yes! It was him, Peter the six-string seer
Still making magic after all those years,
Not by the sea in the land of Honalee,
But under the tents in Texas Hill Country.

Night crept, but as always, morning came
And with it me out taking in the airs
Of Irish jigs and Texas swing when there
Came maestro Peter roaring out my name.

Yes! It was him, Peter the six-string seer
Still making magic after all those years,
Not by the sea in the land of Honalee,
But under the tents in Texas Hill Country.

And there we stood in the summer heat,
Peter saying how sorry, how to blame
He was for being rude, me speechless that
He remembered me, let alone my name.

For five or ten minutes there we were,
Heads bent like flowers not quite gone,
Two dreamers frolicking, blossoming on,
Peter and me together in the Texas sun.

Yes! It was him, Peter the six-string seer
Still making magic after all those years,
Not by the sea in the land of Honalee,
But under the tents in Texas Hill Country.

AIN'T YOU LUCKY?

So you want to know the blues, huh boy? Well, look here,
when Mama up and left that no-good low-life sonofabitch that spring
in Greenweed, Mississippi and skedaddled south to Baton Rouge
and there was never no more horses and hounds and hunts
under the Delta moon, that, boy, was the blues sure and true,
and when not three months later Mama up and left you hunkered
down with Granny and Aunt Vi and skedaddled north back to that
contagious woman-beating peck-o-wood, that was the blues
beneath the blues, blues only the favored few can know.
Now ain't you lucky, boy? I say, ain't you lucky, now you know?

2.

THE ROLLING STONES POEM

Once upon a time gone but not forgotten,
a time perhaps far better forgotten,
there was a man who loved the Rolling Stones,
loved every song they ever cut—all of them.

When young this man loved all things holy,
but more than Jesus and the Holy Ghost
by the time he cleared his twenties he came
to love *Sympathy for the Devil* the most.

Who else but Satan could have understood
his need for drawing blood, actual blood;
who but Satan, as he ticked off one
sin after another, could serve as goad?

So it was, to the long drawn-out wail
of Keith's guitar and Mick's lyrical doom,
he warred, boozed, lusted and doped his way
through late night bars and flophouse rooms.

This man made no claim to anything,
not even a name, and he sure as hell had
no wealth and no good taste except
for the sweet and sour of all things bad.

This man wasn't around when Jesus was,
and he harbored no real doubt,
doubt not being the nature of his game.
He knew about earthly pain and dished it out.

And this man never met a king or a Tsar,
never met the Kennedy's or rode a tank,
and never trapped a troubadour.
But he knew he was a sinner, not a saint,

and laid waste to all the lonely men
hunched over beers in seedy bars
and left broken women in his wake,
stretched out across beds, like scars.

Once upon a time there was this man
who loved the devil of the Rolling Stones
because the devil had sympathy for him.
Who else but Satan could call him home?

JIVING JIMMY CLANTON

No jive I don't know much about Jimmy Clanton
and I don't really remember any of his songs
but I do remember that all the hot young things
in my high school in Baton Rouge back in '58
were nuts about the guy or his music or both

and that was enough for me and even more
for Tommy Smith who not only loved the songs
I can't remember but could play them so exact
you thought he actually was Jimmy Clanton
and looked so much like Clanton that all the hot
young things swooned over him and were ready to
lay down their bodies if not their lives for him

which really rankled all us not so hot young studs
and still would if we thought about it which we
mostly don't because thinking about it does no good
because not one of us back then could play
a Fender let alone sing like Jimmy Clanton the way

Tommy Smith could and besides which Tommy was
cool as cool and Clanton could be and handsome too
with his Brylcreemed black hair double parted
and his black muscle teeshirts and his black jeans
and his come to papa all you hot young things hips
gyrating like Jimmy's and even more like Elvis's

and nothing not even all these decades down the road
can change what really drove us crazy—that
like reportedly Jimmy Clanton Tommy Smith
was on top of everything else not only one cool dude

but one helluva nice guy who liked hanging out
with us and playing pool and not giving a shit

if he lost and Jesus how we hated not
being able to hate him even though he looked
like Jimmy Clanton and played like Jimmy Clanton
and like Jimmy Clanton jiving all the hot young things
with his guitar and with a voice that left them limp
always goddamn him to hell always got the girls.

I, TOO, THOUGHT ERIC CLAPTON WAS GOD

I, too, thought Eric Clapton was God,
and today, listening to a Clapton song,
I think about the me I was when I did.
I was young, I was heady with hope,
I believed in the heart more than the head,
and rock was the lifeblood of the heart.

That was then and this is now,
this drab late-afternoon February day
when clouds grayer than Clapton's face
must have been when he heard his son
had fallen out of an apartment window
to his death advance from the west,
embezzling what's left of day.

I, too, thought Eric Clapton was God,
and today, listening to that Clapton song,
I think about the me I thought I was
when I couldn't justify any old thing,
and any old thing couldn't justify
my belief in anything but belief.

That was then and this is now,
this drab late-afternoon February day
when I still think about the me I was,
but my neighbor's house just burned
and his son in the house burned, too,
and though I'm listening to his song,
Clapton is Clapton, and it gently weeps.

ROY ORBISON IN MACHU PICCHU

It's ridiculous, I know—an American pop
singer, a blue collar blues-voiced
troubadour icon from Texas, Orbison,
the Big O, rooted in rockabilly and country,
plopped down by some trick of mind right
in the middle of those exotic Incan ruins,
all around him the green hills of Cusco,
not the arid plains of Texas, and instead
of longhorns, alpacas and llamas roaming.

But there he is, statue-still and with his
guitar slung across his back like a
black-winged hip archangel, his
dark sunglasses reflecting sacrificial fire,
his hair swept back like the blackened
feathers of a demon condor, protector
of the overworld, and from the black
cauldron of his throat eruptions of sound
so dark it bullies the sun into total eclipse.

The closer to the heavens the city was,
the closer to God and God's mystery,
the Incans believed, and maybe that's it—
the mystery: How, we ask, did the Incans
quarry and carry in those behemoth stone
foundations? How bury their dead
in rock tunnels across a gorge accessible
only by a flimsy rope swing? *How?*

No one knows, but even if we did, there
he stands—Roy Orbison in Machu Picchu,
his god-like jukebox voice booming forth,
echoing off the ancient stones, and snaking
along narrow mountain paths and through

the twists and turns of every passageway;
there he stands, the Caruso of Rock,
the bluesy acoustics of his black six-string
seducing all of Peru; there he stands,
and all I know is, the mystery remains.

WHY I'M SAD ABOUT THE DEATH OF
PAUL REVERE

1938-2014

Not knowing him, I couldn't hate him,
but I could his music—that
damned "Louie Louie" every AM station
on the West Coast seemed to be playing
every other song: *Louie, Louie, Louie...*

Why, then, when I hear on the evening news
that he's dead, am I left so shaken? So sad?

As always, it has to do with a girl,
a girl with big boobs who sat next to me
in Mr. Ludwig's Freshman English I—
not across the sea in Jamaica, a long three
days away by ship, but in Oregon.
Her name? Susie, or Michelle, or Mary Lou.
I don't remember a moon that night,
and there were no roses in her hair,
but there we were, the girl with big boobs
I lusted for constantly and dated once;

there we were, parked in my '50 Chevy
in the college parking lot where,
while I was feeling her up, we were
rockin' to—who else?—Paul Revere
& The Raiders, both of us bouncing up
and down to—what else?—"Louie Louie,"

that soundtrack of my first real sex,
on one October night under Oregon stars
with the first girl whose boobs I laid
hands on, which is why I'm sad—

not just because Paul Revere is dead,
but because that was the once
and only sweetly innocent encounter
I could ever have, there in my gray Chevy
with the girl from Freshman English I
under me and "Louie Louie" booming out
across a parking lot not yet paved over.

THE POEM ABOUT THE BEATLES

Revolver, Rubber Soul, Sgt. Pepper's, The Beatles,
Abbey Road, Let It Be—Don't get me wrong,
I love them, too. As they were for millions,
they were the soundtrack of the sex-desperate,
id-intoxicated, acne-riddled adolescent me.

Here comes the sun, they sang, and I believed,
opening myself like a window, rain and snow
no hindrance, knowing the sun would win out
in the end, the end not something I could fathom,
one of their LPs an antidote to no tomorrow.

Let it be, they sang, and I believed that, too,
never doubting that I would always have a mast
to tie myself to, that the yellow submarine
would welcome me aboard, would take me
on its magical mystery cruise, would let *me* be.

But this is the poem about the Beatles that
I never wrote, and now there are more
yesterdays than tomorrows, more time spent
in port than on those rainbowed seas,
George and John dead, Paul and Ringo old.

I'm old, too, and now I know I am the walrus,
goo goo g'joob, I'm the old man on the hill,
I'm Rocky Raccoon, I'm Gideon without his bible.
I'm old, too, and now I know that the truth
might not set me free, but that the truth is free.

Truth is, when I first heard the Beatles I hated
their *I wanna hold your hand...yeah, yeah, yeah.*
Jesus, oh Jesus Christ, I said—not that again.

And *working like a dog/...sleeping like a log?*
How could they get away with such claptrap?

I do believe that Lucy in the sky with diamonds
could be LSD, but I'm old now, older than sixty-four,
and in the poem about the Beatles my road is short
and winding, and while on a good day I believe
the sun will always come, I know it also goes.

THE MAN WHO WANTED TO BE CARLOS SANTANA

Oye como va—Listen, this is how it is.
I know Santana is Santa Ana, contracted.
But that has nothing to do with it.
I'm not military—was in fact one
of those long-haired hipsters in the Sixties,
and being an American, I wouldn't idolize
a Mexican general, even if I liked generals,
which I don't. And no, it isn't that Latin
fueled guitar, though I mastered major chords
when I was fourteen and no different than
any American kid in imagining myself
as Clapton or Page or any of a dozen more
guitar gods. Partly it's the man himself.
It's Carlos, so cool so smooth so mysterious,
like the magical realism I learned about
in my Spanish Lit class in college.
That Carlos, not just Carlos the guitar god.
Then there's the women. Who wouldn't want
to know who the real sultry woman is,
the one who modeled that black magic mama
and her evil ways. That Carlos, too.
Mostly, though, a student of language myself,
to be able to speak, to sing in not one
but two different tongues, to mix them
like James Bond his drinks, only in Carlos' case
shaken *and* stirred—that's way past cool,
as if the Fonz, James Dean and Bond were one
and the same: a Cuban stogie and a stick
of dynamite, an Uzi and an atom bomb.
I know Santana is Santa A-n-n-a, too,
but neither saints nor angels need apply here.
I'll bet magic women melt the polar icecaps
before global warming can make advances.
And I'll bet Carlos always gets the girl.

NO OTHER WIZARD: ZIGGY STARDUST IN ST. PETER'S CELESTIAL REHAB CENTER

My God! Only sixty-nine, and here he is,
checking in, at the mercy of winged masseurs.
Or we *think* it's him. Without the over the top
makeup, multicolored tight jumpsuits and mass
of flame-red hair, how can we be sure?

More emaciated than androgynous,
in his white shirt, black waistcoat and trousers,
and with his slicked-back blond hair,
he looks like he's just risen from the dead,
which we know is but a foolish human myth.

No wonder some of us still wonder
if he's really Ziggy, our glam-rock Liberace,
troubadour of Tinsel Town: He's so thin
he's thinner than the Thin White Duke,
and those bags under his eyes and that
shattered visage. And that last video:
him on his deathbed singing so eerily,
his bandaged eyes already closed to light.

But he really is Ziggy, the same Ziggy
who could charm the Dark Angel himself,
all that fame embalming him like his hordes
of female fans as unmistakable as this
halfway house to either Heaven or Hell,
Halloween Jack and Major Tom, Aladdin Sane
and Jareth the Goblin King long ago
shed like so many outdated snake skins.

They say he kept his urine in the fridge
so no other wizard could use it to enchant him.
What other wizard? He was his own wizard,

enchanted by his own super-sized concoctions
of voodoo telegenic mayhem and magic.

Look at that spectral face. It's Ziggy, all right.
Ziggy to the cancerous end—that harpy eating
at his liver. Good thing he joined us here,
but sad, too. He never saw his golden years.
God only knows what they would have been.

ELVIS SIGHTING IN THE ARTHUR CRUDUP OLD AGE HOME

Like they say, what you see is what you get,
and mostly Velvet Elvis is what we got.
But what we saw wasn't what we thought
we'd see. Who knew? Who knew a mama's boy
had so much contrariness deep inside of him?

Mostly he was all Deep South pc—polite,
soft-spoken, even humble, believe it or not.
Mostly we liked him, even at eighty
and by then wasting away, all that fat
oozing off his body like runny biscuit dough,
and halfway ugly, too, until he smiled—
you know, that half-curl smile he had,
that *come on mama* slick willie smile
that lit up more than just a movie screen.

Mostly, we say, because whenever he had
a hankering for something—say one of his
peanut butter and banana concoctions,
or someone to fetch a certain pink teddy bear
from Graceland, one about as battered
and old as him—Christ, how he could turn,
one minute purring like a Cadillac and the next
nasty as chitlin odor stinking up a house.

Singing, we reckoned, would have helped him,
but by then that bugle-blue voice of his
couldn't carry any kind of tune, not
even one of those scripture-soaked,
rapturous gospel hullabaloos he loved so much,
or even a genuine down on the Delta blues,
though he tried, bless his heart, gripping his IV
like a mic and blurting out a few notes he
couldn't hold, a sweat-clumped scarf of sound.

So singing was out and with nothing much
left for him to do but ogle the nurses, eat
and watch tv, images flashing like Vegas lights,
he could sull up worse than a possum when
he didn't get his way, working that lip
the way he did an audience, eyes harder than
a karate kick, though mostly he didn't say
too much, figuring, we suspected, that he'd said
it all—in living, in the movies, in his songs.

Then it happened—one day he turned his face
to the wall, and that was all she wrote. He died,
but just before he did, we heard half hummed,
half whispered like air from a tire on its way
to being flat, *Well, that's all right now mama...
that's all right ... I'm leaving town for sure ...*

And what we thought we'd see we did:
that Mississippi mama's boy, that Tupelo
troubadour, that Memphis mafioso of music
remastering his first song with his last breath.

REALLY, ELTON

That you were gay had nothing at all to do
with my not having written about you,
not at first. I hadn't even known you were gay.
But later? I mean, Elton—*really?* Those
bigger than I'd ever seen rose-colored glasses,
and that multi-colored frock? My god,
you looked as if you'd just stepped out
of Sergeant Pepper's or the Yellow Submarine,
or the worst hallucination I'd ever had.

That was the you I first encountered,
not the more thoroughly in the closet you,
the you you hid so well. I have to say,
when I became aware you were in fact gay,
I wasn't really flabbergasted or put off.
I think I always suspected, somehow.
The glasses, the frock…just validated what
I felt, but was afraid to think, I knew.

Really, Elton, to be the Mississippi macho boy
I imagined I was supposed to be,
I tried to despise you for what you were,
a gay man or back then what we called queer,
or worse. A modicum of ill at ease was all
I could muster, and even that dissolved
to mere mirage, like early morning mist
over a lake when the sun works its magic—
the sun your rockin' keyboard and the stutter
of your voice on "B-Bennie and the Jets."

So no, I've never written about you, Elton,
and I apologize for not having done so,
but please know it wasn't by design,
merely a long lapse of inspiration. Now,

with this epistle, that sin of omission has,
I hope, no sway—not now, when both of us,
minus the glasses and the frock, are closing in
on the end of the yellow brick road, the *real* end,
for which there are no closing credits.

3.

STRANGE ENTANGLEMENTS

Hey, Bobby, something's blowin' in the wind,
you can hear it thrashing and I ain't talking trees.
It's here and it's everywhere, from Rio to Rome,
Innsbruck to Istanbul, from Kenya to Kathmandu,
Barrow to Beijing, from Düsseldorf to Duluth.
It clogs the rivers running through our dreams,
clogs Bethel Woods and Newport and the Village,
clogs Grand Central, and Ground Zero, too.
Something's blowin', Bob, and it ain't flowers
flogged by wind in Central Park; it's the darkness
of below, it's subterranean blue and blacker than
the blight at their roots, their stems, their petals.
Something's blowin', Robert, leaving in its wake
these strange entanglements of light and dark.

EARLY MORNING AT THE WEST SIDE Y

For Glenn Raucher

My God! The man with long white hair
waiting for an elevator on the thirteenth floor
is Edgar Winter, blear-eyed from a night
spent raising the roof at the Fillmore East.
Maybe we're seeing things, maybe we're
still high on the Sixties. But no, it really
is him, Edgar Winter in the flesh. There
are calluses on his fingers, his pupils
are musical notes. We follow him
down to the small café off the lobby,
stand behind him in the buffet line,
and take the small square black table
adjacent to his, an intermittent cool
breeze blowing in through the window.
For a half hour we sip our coffee,
nibble on muffins, and out of the corners
of our eyes watch The Legend sip his,
simultaneously skimming through the *Times*.
They don't believe in superstition here,
we remind ourselves, picturing him standing
before the window on the thirteenth floor,
Central Park below him, and beyond
Manhattan's skyline, spectral and beautiful.
Superstition is as dead as the architect
of this old building and there is no such
thing as ghosts and this is Edgar Winter,
but when he pushes his long white hair
back, deposits his paper coffee cup
in a trash receptacle, and shuffles out
and disappears among the excruciatingly
New York faces floating down 63rd Street,
we are dismayed. Superstition is dead,
but everywhere we look there are ghosts.

THE DAY AFTER RAY MANZAREK DIED

The day after Ray Manzarek died,
upstate New York was sunny and warm
when I started driving home from Troy,
but by the time I pulled into my driveway,
Jesus, I said to myself, Oh Jesus Christ.

Black clouds had snuffed out the sun,
the wind wailing like Morrison, hail
the size of knuckles drumming double
time, and thunder throbbing like
psychotic keyboards stopped in
mid-run by the downbeat of the sun.
And there was warmth again, and light.
Jesus, I said to myself, Oh Jesus Christ.

ODE TO BILLY JOEL

This June morning, driving east to Vermont
and then northeast to New Hampshire
and the White Mountains home of Robert Frost,
I was in an upstate New York state of mind.

Hash browns, bagels, two eggs over easy,
cheddar sharp, waffles with New York maple syrup—
those were what I was turning over
in my New York mind, plus cups of Empire bold.

By the time I rolled into west Brattleboro
and turned north, food was out and fasting in,
pickups and clunkers instead of fancy cars,
the *Brattleboro Reformer*, not the *New York Times*.

Five o'clock came and went, mountains bulged
and I could say rhyme is highly suspect
in our time, but still your song played on.
By dusk I was in a Robert Frost state of mind.

ODE TO CHUCK E. BERRY

Chuck duckwalked out today and Maybellene,
oh Maybellene sits on top of the hill
grieving her hot little Cadillac Coupe de Ville:

Out there it's blue blue skies and talcum clouds;
in here it's stains and rips and dirty glass.
Out there it's twenty degrees and full of sass;
in here it's seventy degrees and black as shrouds.

Chuck duckwalked out today and Maybellene,
oh Maybellene done traded in her Coupe de Ville…

Chuck duckwalked out today and Johnny B. Goode,
oh Johnny B. Goode stands in his cabin of earth & wood
among the evergreens way back up in the woods:

Out there it's blue blue skies and talcum clouds;
in here it's gray gray walls and filthy glass.
Out there it's twenty degrees and full of sass;
in here it's seventy degrees and black as shrouds.

Chuck duckwalked out today and Johnny B. Goode
done hung up his guitar, done hung it up for good …

Chuck duckwalked out today and sweet Nadine,
oh sweet Nadine gets in her coffee colored Cadillac
and seeing what she sees can never double back:

Out there it's blue blue skies and talcum clouds;
in here it's stains and rips and shattered glass.
Out there it's twenty degrees and full of sass;
in here it's seventy degrees and black as shrouds.

Chuck duckwalked out today and sweet Nadine,
oh sweet Nadine was last seen motorin' over the hill …

SORRY, ROD

Here it is, the first full day of summer
and *Maggie Mae* blaring away
on my car radio, and singing along
with Rod at the top of my morning lungs,
how can I help but think of her,
the girl in the cool white Mustang
cruising past where I was hanging on
in the park at Mountain Ave and Main.

Forty years is a long time to have
to forget the Molotov of anger and pain
she lobbed at me out the window
as she drove away—forever it turned out.
Sorry, Rod, but I wasn't led away
from home, I wasn't used, wasn't blind,
wasn't anybody's fool, and it wasn't me
kicked in the head. I wrecked the bed.

But it's summer now, the sun still gentle,
wind still mild, and while I'm sorry
about the kicking, I'm not about having seen
her face that first time forty years ago,
and not that I can see it still as clearly as
that dim smudge of moon in this blue sky.
Here's to her, my mother of a lover, the girl
in the white Mustang, oh my Maggie Mae.

JOHN LENNON IN A LAMBORGHINI

The moon landing was in fact a fake,
the earth *is* actually flat, and McCartney
really did die. Everybody knows this,
and I know Lennon lives. How do I know?

Call it karma, if you wish, call it crazy,
but I know because I just saw Lennon
rolling past the Dakota in a Lamborghini.
It was white, like Lennon's suit,

and on the license plates IMAGINE was
flashing pink, then blue, then green.
I know what you're thinking, that I've been
imbibing too much. Lennon was murdered,

and he's deader than strawberry fields
in winter. Yes, but have another toke
and imagine if you can: Chapman missed.
Strawberry fields … *forever.* Remember?

LOVE ME DO, BABY, LOVE ME DO

I'm white-haired now but so are they, those lads,
the two that are left, one the drummer who
replaced me. Back then we all had black hair
that glistened in the stage lights in the clubs
we played in Liverpool, and later in Hamburg.
God, what a raffish lot we were, but the music
was the best we ever played. Even they admit that.
Hamburg was wild, and so were we, carrying on
on stage sometimes for thirty hours a week,
sometimes even more. They wanted savageness,
the Germans, and brother we gave it to them.
I beat the hell out of the drums, and the guitars,
man, they screamed like men being tortured.
Chuck Berry never sounded so good,
and as for Duane Eddy, he was nobody!
Hendrix—he would've fit right in. Two years,
that's how long it lasted, how long *I* lasted.
Without so much as a by-your-leave they
dumped me. August 16, it was—1962.
Aston, our manager, called me into his office,
delivered the news. They weren't even there.
You bloody well know I was pissed, but more
stunned than anything. It left me with a sickness
in my mouth, not least because I didn't know why.
I still don't. And no, it hadn't anything at all
to do with my being better looking, as rumour
has it, even now after all these years. Or maybe
it did. Who knows. I know I was good enough.
Bloody hell, I was the number one drummer
in Liverpool at the time. Maybe it was Aston.
Maybe he just didn't like me. Does it matter?
And as for what might have been—that game—
look at what is: I'm healthy, happy, married
forty years, have two beautiful daughters,

four grandkids, and unlike two of them,
I'm not dead. For a while I worked in a bakery,
retired from civil service after thirty years,
that's true. But I've always had my music.
Now I'm doing a world tour, there's talk
of movies, and I'm putting out a new album
early next year. I'm not one of them,
but they're not me. I have to live with it,
of course, but I do. And when someone bitches
about how unfair they think life has been
to them, I smile and say: You could do worse,
you could be me. But then, I always favoured
the ironic touch. Love me do, baby, love me do.

THE FAB FOUR IN FROST COUNTRY

They save the song I always hated for last,
this Beatles look-alike and more or less
sound-alike band, this fifth-year here
in Frost country counterfeit Liverpudlian band,
this Fab Four rockin' razzmatazz Nehru jacket
Dr. Pepper's not so lonely heartfelt band.

Watching them, I wonder what Frost would think,
the old poet with Mt. Rushmore visage Frost.
I doubt he would want to hold my hand,
and though he might shout, words would be
the only things he'd want to twist,
much as he did long after he was sixty-four.

After the band unplugs, the fireworks start,
lighting the sky to a super gamma ray explosion
of colorful star stuff and the crowd
mobbing the soccer field to a ghostly glow,
a writhing emanation, but what captures me
is the satellite glinting like a silver crucifix
in the southern part of the sky. It transfixes me.

The year 2000 has long come and gone,
satellites plentiful and mostly ignored—
just there, like the moon and stars, like the sun.
And I think Frost, with one eye fixed firmly
on that satellite and one on the fireworks,

would, like deaf Beethoven, roll over and over,
while covering his ears, while wrinkling his nose.

TWENTY-SEVEN

Hendrix. Joplin. Cobain. Morrison. Now,
Winehouse. What is it about this number,
twenty-seven? This nothing number?
What significance did it ever have?
My mother was born in 1927, though not
on the twenty-seventh. But so what?
It could have been 1926, and almost was.

The only numbers I ever mastered
weren't numbers—they were letters,
all those little, mysterious letters
in equations. Algebra was the only math
I liked, and the only high school math
I more than just passed: not A,
but B was mastery enough for me.

I don't believe in the magic of numbers:
that seven always means good luck,
that a thirteenth floor is a good thing
to omit from any architectural design,
that six of one and half a dozen of another
are the same; and as for sixty-nine,
that old satanic sign, the hell with it.

Things might or might not be cheaper
by the dozen, but sex gets a pass,
sixty-nine in its case dripping magic;
and triumvirates and trinities aside,
three is a number with real clout,
structuring everything from fairy tales
to Hegel, atoms, pop music and jokes.

But twenty-seven? All right, so there are
twenty-seven books in the New Testament

and twenty-seven generations from David
to Jesus, twenty-seven Hebrew letters.
For Morrison and the others did this matter?
As a lunar sign, if it means light in darkness,
light lost. The Bible uses it six times.

DRUMMING ARMAGEDDON

I, too, have friends dead from drugs,
guys I hung out with on my hometown streets
and in the war memorial park with wood railings
we kept falling off, too stoned to balance on.

There was Zak, the lumberjack-looking redhead
who was dumb and because he was dumb
an unwitting victim of fun: He dosed on smack,
thinking he could take it, but it taking him;

and Allen, a doper of the first order who
made it into early middle age, then
did himself in with mixtures of booze and crack,
his body rotting behind the butcher shop;

then there was Herbie, sweetly temperate Herbie
who dreamed of being a ferocious drummer
and high on Ginger Baker riffs and weed,
gigged out on the front end of an 18-wheeler.

There are others, but when I hear a car or truck
backfire, when I hear raindrops on a roof
or distant rolls of thunder, when I hear
the neighbor's boy drumming night into dawn,

it's Zak and Allen I think of, and Herbie,
Herbie twirling his sticks high over his head,
then ripping into classic Cream, Ginger
at his side, drumming Armageddon into exile.

WHO REMEMBERS HERBIE?

I will die in this body.
—*Maudelle Driskell*

It was the year of street corners and drugs,
of moonlit midnight trips in the cemetery,
of angry wives and neglected kids;
the year of cops and constant dread
of being busted, of smack and methadone.
The year of overdoses and dead friends.

Herbie, for one. But not of drugs.
Herbie died on the business end
of a semi, him and his band mates,
on a two-lane blacktop one hundred
and fifty miles from home; died
coming back from a gig, maybe
happy, maybe a little high on weed.

So many maybes, so many what ifs.
Only two things for certain: Herbie
was nineteen and a really good kid,
never uptight, never more stubborn than
he had to be, never stoned on anything
but a little homegrown and that rarely;

and he was a damned good drummer
dreaming of a future octaves higher
than his present, dreaming of being
like Ginger Baker, or being Ginger Baker.
Man, he could pound those skins!

Herbie lived in his body, died in his body,
and forty summers after the year of street
corners and drugs, Herbie's body lies
in the cemetery swaddled in moonlight.

Those are the facts. Do they matter? If so,
to whom? And to what purpose, if any?

Once upon a time Herbie lived in his body,
and now he doesn't. Those are the facts.
Who will induct him into the Rock & Roll
Hall of the Forgotten? And does it matter?
Oh, the singular melody of questions.
Oh, the drum roll of impossible answers.

I KNOW YOU'RE IN DETROIT

August 13, 2018

Dear Aretha, I know you're in Detroit and I'm here,
miles and miles away, but I'd like to apologize,
before it's too late. You're on your deathbed,
that's pretty clear, surrounded as you are
by family and friends, and the national press
in the trenches already, sensing a headline. Poems
like this are more personal than public eulogies,
and for the most part not even close to being a blip
on most Americans' consciousness. So my apology is
between us, which is proper and more poignant.

Aretha, I apologize for having never written a poem
for or about you, not in all the Hit Parades of years
I've grooved to you and your soulful music. I admit,
I've written many about many of your peers,
some equal to you in their various musical ways,
some not even close. I apologize, I really do,
but know this, dear Aretha: Even as you lie bedridden
there in the shadow of Motown, this latecomer poem,
unlike any others I might have written, catalogs nothing
less than the entire opus of the entirely beautiful you.

TUNING THE RADIO

When I was young and my car old
the radio had only two dials,
one for volume and one for tuning.
Song to song I hunted for stations,
the tuning dial spinning like a planet
in my limber fingers, Easy Listening
and Country and Classical and Jazz
jettisoned, hot Rock my only balm.

By the time the Sixties comet fizzled
there was pre-set, buttons to punch.
And punch I did, still fixed on Rock,
and I don't mean the Pop kind either,
my engine fueled by the hallucinogens
of organ and guitar, the percussive uppers
of drums, the throbbing downer of bass,
the shrieking overdose of violin.

Now I have the rapid orbit of the Scan,
the ultra-speedy, station-locking Seek
at my command. Too late. These days
I decline, setting the dial in my blue car
at 88.3, 96.7, 106.5 and leaving it there,
whatever comes my digital way—Marley,
Mozart, Clooney, Dylan, Williams, Bird—
acceptable, now I'm old and my car young.

BOVINE BOP

One evening Charlie Parker stood
on a country road and like
a wolf lifting its muzzle raised
his sax to the night sky

and blew a tune so godalmighty hot
the cow to which he played
spat out its cud and tore
the pasture up doing the bovine bop.

ABOUT THE AUTHOR

George Drew is the author of eight poetry collections, with *Pastoral Habits: New and Selected Poems*, *Down & Dirty* and *The View From Jackass Hill*, winner of the 2010 X.J. Kennedy Poetry Prize, all from Texas Review Press. His eighth, *Fancy's Orphan*, appeared in 2017 with Tiger Bark Press. *Drumming Armageddon* is his ninth collection. Recently George won the Knightville Poetry Contest, *The New Guard*, his poem appearing in the 2017 edition, and two other poems as Honorable Mention in the Steve Kowit Poetry Contest, appeared in the *2018 and 2019 San Diego Poetry Anthology*. He was a recipient of the Bucks County Muse Award in 2016 for contributions to the Bucks County PA literary community. Recently, one of his poems from *Fancy's Orphan* appeared in *Verse Daily*. George's biography will appear in *Mississippi Poets: A Literary Guide*, University of Mississippi Press, edited by Catherine Savage Brosman.